LOVING EARTH

SOME STARTING POINTS FOR EARTHCARE

AN ALPHABET BOOK

Loving Earth Project

lovingearth-project.uk

WELCOME

We all care about someone, somewhere, or something. If they are sick we can look after them; if they are threatened we can defend them. Environmental changes are already damaging many parts of the world and threatening others; many of us are anxiously wondering what can be done.

The Loving Earth Project offers some starting points. The project aims to help people engage creatively with some of these big questions and without being overwhelmed. We can start from any point – any letter of the alphabet – focusing on something that we care about and taking some kind of action to help care for its future. This book showcases 26 textile panels (each 30×30cm) made by a range of different people. Each panel illustrates something the panel-maker loves, how it's threatened, or what they are doing about it. Making textile art takes time and care, and this has helped the panel-makers to reflect more deeply, learn about the issues, decide what to do to help, and then spread the word to encourage others.

Most governments and organisations have been too slow to act; it's up to all of us to do so. Small actions matter. They may range from personal changes in daily habits, to finding out more, talking to people, spiritual and campaigning responses, or creating textile art works. One step may then lead to another.

You can see the Loving Earth questions on page 56 of this booklet. We hope they will be helpful to you as well. Taking a first step from a narrow initial focus, we can often learn and gain confidence to continue the journey, and work with others to become part of the solution.

So far, over 400 textile panels have been made, by people in many parts of the world, ranging from young children to the very elderly. You can see most of them on our website, **lovingearth-project.uk**, along with more information about the project. Each panel in this book is accompanied by a short quote from the panel-maker, along with a different short comment on the theme.

We are all connected and depend on each other, through the complex web of life on Earth. We hope this project inspires you to take action to care for the future of what you love, and of us all.

Rici Marshall Cross, **Linda Murgatroyd**, **Matt Rosen**
Quaker Arts Network, January 2022

A AWARENESS

"How can we protect nature and ourselves as part of nature? Capitalism destroys human and other nature, so awareness of this is key. I've improperly sewn a white heart, but I like that. My mother helped me; she has been sewing by hand for many years. What's important is awareness and connection. These bring joy to the planet."

This panel shows an attempt to connect to the source of life, but it is imperfect, perhaps wounded. It's important to be aware, as the panel-maker is, that human activity, especially if it is driven by greed, or the lust for power, can damage and destroy humans, other creatures and their communities and habitats

If we are aware of the consequences of our actions we can be open to new possibilities and choose to act in different ways. We can choose to become healers, to work from our deepest values, such as love or other spiritual values. We can help to heal the world, and in doing so may be healed ourselves.

B BEES

"This piece was inspired by the Government authorising the use of neonicotinoid pesticides on sugar beet. This could have a devastating effect on bees and insect populations in general. Clearly, if we lose our pollinators, we are in serious trouble. In my garden, I have a range of bee friendly shrubs and flowers which provide nectar throughout the season. I have bog beans in March, flowering cherries in April and May, and buddleias which are coming into flower and were covered in bees yesterday... and I don't use any form of pesticides."

Insect populations have declined sharply in recent decades, as agriculture has become an industrial process. Large farms have replaced areas previously occupied by wild flowering plants. Pesticide use has greatly increased, even though it can kill pollinating insects. Successive generations of insecticides have been banned, but usually only after several decades. By this time they have already seriously damaged many species and habitats, and reduced biodiversity.

Save the bees

Plant Flowers

Create Habitats

C COWS

"I love to see cows in green meadows, ruminating peacefully. However, cows create methane, a very damaging greenhouse gas. There are over a billion cattle in the world, and the number has increased due to beef and dairy demand. Rearing cattle often means destroying forests and planting swaths of monocultures. Further environmental damage results from transporting cattle. Industrial beef production results in biodiversity loss and doesn't give cattle decent lives. I stopped eating meat, and I'm cutting down on dairy products. We urgently need better agriculture policies too."

Worldwide, cattle are the top agricultural source of greenhouse gasses. Methane from cattle is 28 times more damaging to the climate than carbon dioxide with respect to climate change. Beef production also takes up a vast amount of land, which is often overgrazed and degraded. We can lessen global emissions substantially by changing our diets to avoid beef and dairy products.

D DARN IT

"I mend clothes. It connects me to my mum, who regularly settled down to do the darning. I'm celebrating the darns by making them into decorations. We can make a difference by extending the lives of our clothes, even by months. We can lessen our contributions to landfills, and lessen our carbon, water, and waste footprints. Engaging with the Love Your Clothes campaign can help us make the most of our clothing."

We're all consumers. But there's a difference between consumerism (overconsumption) and having enough to live well. By mending things and buying less or more carefully we can reduce our environmental impact. Repairing our clothing is part of this work. Let's try to live simply so that other people and species can simply live!

E ENERGY

"Renewables, and wind energy in particular, provide an increasing proportion of our energy. This allows us to stop using fossil fuels, which have contributed so much to global warming. The UK is the sixth largest wind power producer in the world and has targets to produce a lot more. I have switched to an all-renewable energy supplier, and I have put some savings into community wind power projects."

We can reduce our energy use in many ways, such as insulating our homes, buying energy-efficient appliances, and travelling less, especially avoiding planes and cars. For the energy that we do use, we need to replace coal, oil, and gas with energy from renewable sources such as the wind, sun, hydroelectricity or tides. Does your home energy tariff provide you with 100% renewable electricity?

We can make some changes ourselves but regulations are the most effective way to achieve high standards in energy efficiency. There are many challenges, and investment in research, public education and energy infrastructure is essential.

F FIRE

"I love the moors above my home... Droughts caused by climate change dry out the peat and leave these wonderful spaces vulnerable to wildfires. Fires destroy the peat, releasing the carbon, which in turn worsens climate change. My panel features the angel Gabby, whose rainbow wings celebrate the diversity of all creation. She is the angel of hope and change; as she flies out from the fires, she is scattering the seeds of a green renewal."

———————————————

Climate change has had a profound impact on the frequency and scale of wildfires in many parts of the globe, including in Australia, the Arctic, and parts of Europe, and North America. Fires are destroying habitats and killing large numbers of wildlife and people, probably leading to many species extinctions. Both wildfires and intentional burning of forests, garbage, and fossil fuels add to the spiral of global heating releasing more carbon and other pollutants into the atmosphere.

G GROWTH

"Traditional economics has assumed that our goals are profit and growth. But continual growth in GDP isn't sustainable in a finite world. Social, economic, and ecological justice are also important. We need to rethink priorities and consider what kind of economy will allow life on earth to flourish – an economy that prioritizes clean air, water, and biodiversity. I've been struggling with this for some time, and I've found the Doughnut Economics approach exciting and helpful both in personal decisions, and in conversations about government policy."

Doughnut economics is a doughnut-shaped visual framework for sustainable development, created by economist Kate Raworth. On the outside, there are planetary boundaries, beyond which lies the risk of catastrophic environmental change. On the inside, there are social boundaries, beyond which people lack access to essential resources like healthcare and education. It helps us understand how an economy and society can thrive without surpassing the planet's ecological limits.

fresh thinking for flourishing

ECOLOGICAL CEILING

air pollution   ozone layer depletion

SOCIAL FOUNDATION

biodiversity loss

land conversion

SHORTFALL

ocean acidification

OVERSHOOT

thriving economy

freshwater withdrawals

chemical pollution

nitrogen and phosphorus loading

doughnut economics

H HOME GROWN

"I've always loved gardening. As a child, I helped my dad, who gave me my own vegetable plot. And since then, I've really enjoyed growing vegetables: for freshness, for variety... Both of my children are keen gardeners now, and we've started a community garden in a deprived area which has been going strong for six years. I just can't stop!"

Buying seasonal fruits and vegetables grown locally can significantly reduce our carbon emissions. Organic food is generally best for biodiversity and health and causes the lowest greenhouse gas emissions. Growing your own fruits and vegetables organically is best of all, as it eliminates the carbon required to ship produce, cuts back on food waste, and helps us connect to nature. Start with small plants that grow easily where you live, and choose ones that grow vertically if space is tight. Consider fruit trees if you have land. Even producing a fraction of what you eat can make a big difference, and it can be a whole lot of fun.

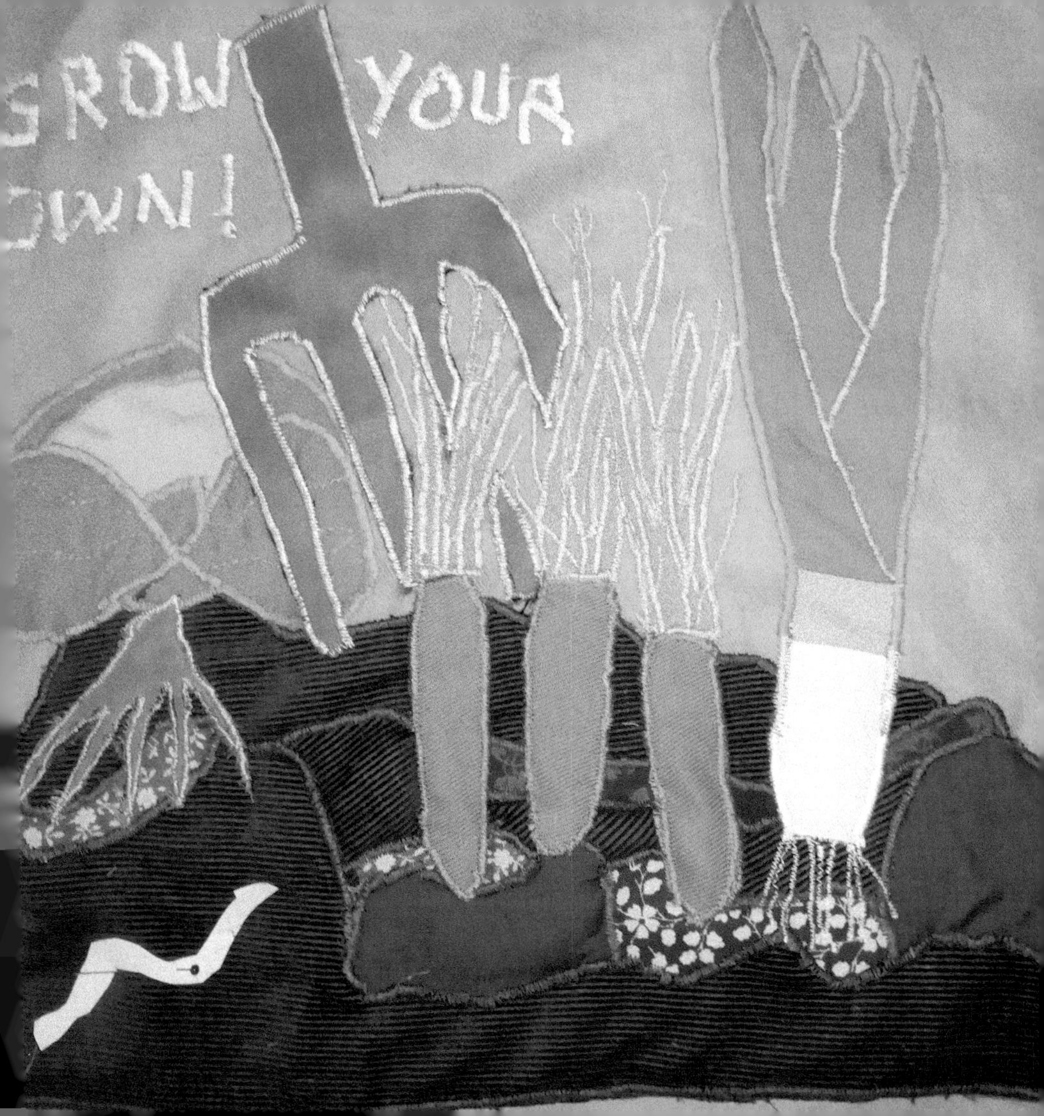
GROW YOUR
OWN!

ICE

"Human activity contributes a great deal to global warming, and the resulting rising temperatures are melting ice in the poles. This threatens the animals living near the poles. It also endangers those living in coastal regions, where flooding and erosion are concerns. This is fundamentally a political problem and governments should fund alternative energy sources, protect ecosystems, and work to adapt how we live."

Climate change has had a greater warming effect on the Arctic and Antarctic than other parts of the world and we could see ice-free summers in the Arctic by 2040. Glaciers in the mountains are also melting faster than ever, resulting in mudfalls and more frequent droughts and famines downstream. Loss of habitat threatens many species with extinction and this is exacerbated by oil and mineral extraction. Sea levels are predicted to rise by a further 15-25cm by 2050, threatening islands and coastal regions. Icemelt also makes global warming accelerate, as less heat is reflected from the sun and methane is released from frozen ground, so there is really no time to lose. We need both to protect polar regions, and to help the communities affected.

J JUSTICE

"Those with the least power and fewest resources suffer the most from the effects of climate change. This is most evident in the Global South. Africa is the continent most vulnerable to climate change, while contributing the least to that change's causes. That is a substantial injustice. My panel represents initiatives to relieve food poverty at the global and local levels. I wanted to picture our unity across continents: there's no 'other' in this crisis."

Climate Justice is an understanding that climate change is entangled with issues of human rights, economic and social justice and inequity. It has been a key focus at UN Climate Conferences since 2000. Since then, the paradigm of climate justice has been taken up by grassroots movements and religions around the world. They urge us to focus on how climate change creates and worsens other social injustices and inequalities and address these issues together.

K KIDS

"Too many city kids are cut off from the natural world. They live in flats with no safe outdoor places to play. They have nowhere to muck about with mud, earth, and wild creatures. This has been exacerbated during the pandemic as children are confined to their homes and isolated. Walking the local streets, I realized how many wild places have recently been paved over. That moved me to plant flowers around my street, and I'm exploring rewilding local parks so children can play."

In cities around the world, children whose future has already been jeopardized by global climate change suffer from what Richard Louv calls 'nature-deficit disorder'. Fortunately, this is an area where we can make a difference in our communities. We can help kids get outside and connect to what needs protecting by planting gardens, restoring parks, preventing over-development, and ensuring access to outdoor play. Mud, earth, and wild creatures could and should be part of every childhood.

L LOVE

"I care deeply for our suffering polluted but still stunningly beautiful planet. I procrastinated making a panel for many weeks but finally shrugged off my fear of failure... I wanted to buy nothing new. I used the old cushion covers for the orange base and backing. I retrieved a box of buttons that my late mother had collected over many years. For the blue circle I used a school uniform polo shirt from one of my granddaughters... This work has given me enormous pleasure."

Inspired by love, we can each use what we have to care for the world. Some of us can repair clothes, others have spades, money, land or time to listen, others can access information. Acting out of love is more effective than acting out of fear, and it can also sustain us inwardly, especially if we work together. That is the inspiration for the Loving Earth Project and all for the beautiful panels in this book. It's also the inspiration for the Climate Coalition's "Show the Love" campaign, every February – look out for the green hearts, or create some of your own.

MOTHS

"Moths are very sensitive to change and play a vital role in our environment. A sizable drop in the moth population has affected many other species. However moths can recover quickly if we improve their environment... We can all contribute by planting flowers, volunteering, or fundraising."

Moths are rather beautiful, but because many are nocturnal, they are often not appreciated as much as butterflies. Moths also have a central role in many ecosystems, as pollinators and as food for many other creatures. However they are in sharp decline because of climate change, pesticides and other pollutants. The sublime Garden Tiger moth used to be a familiar sight in England's gardens but its numbers have fallen by around 90% in recent decades. So it's vital that we help moths by conserving their habitats, limiting our carbon emissions to slow climate change, and stop using harmful chemicals.

N NET ZERO

"Earth has been facing disaster for far too long. We need to make a stand for systemic transformation to halt climate change and biodiversity loss. Sustainable and creative responses are needed to enable transition to a life-sustaining society for all... To go forward, we need to value interdependence and live more simply and slowly."

Net zero carbon dioxide (CO_2) emissions means that the same amount of CO_2 is taken out of the air as is released into it by human activity. Excess CO_2 and other 'greenhouse gas' emissions means too much warmth is trapped in the atmosphere. To avoid the worst effects of climate change, global temperatures must not rise more than 1.5°C compared to temperatures around the year 1800. To achieve this, scientists worldwide recommend that global emissions need to fall by about 45% by the year 2030 (compared to 2010) and reach net zero around 2050. Only radical changes can do this; how can we find and encourage the leadership to make this happen?

O OCEANS

"My panel is inspired by 'Barney', a humpback whale seen regularly in the Firth of Forth this winter. Globally, humpbacks are increasing because there is less hunting, but they still face many dangers, such as entanglement with ropes from fishing boats, and eating rubbish, mostly plastic. We must find ways of re-using/recycling plastic more, and reducing single-use plastic. I've tried to reduce my reliance on plastic, by bulk-buying products in larger containers, and by recycling. My next action is to try products without plastic packaging such as solid shampoo bars."

Micro and nano sized particles of plastic, too small to be seen, are the most dangerous as they infiltrate all ecosystems including rivers and oceans. Many countries are trying to ban these, but it is complicated. We can reduce/refuse plastic, but safe ways to dispose of it have not yet been found, and plastic recycling has limited effect. Climate change is also making seawater more acidic, and industrial fishing methods and oil spills are decimating marine environments. Greenpeace estimates that *at least* 30% of our oceans need to be protected by 2030 to halt this decline.

P PEAT

"Peatlands are thought to be the most efficient carbon sinks on earth... When peat is extracted, it releases a lot of carbon dioxide into the atmosphere. Peat accumulates very slowly, so it's vital that we protect peatlands... I now buy peat-free compost and am starting to make my own. I also support a campaign to use only peat-free products."

Peat is a special type of soil created when plants decompose in waterlogged conditions, without enough oxygen or nutrients. Peatlands (also known as moors, bogs, peat swamp forests, permafrost tundra, muskegs or fens) are found in all continents. They are home to many rare plants, insects and birds. They cover just 3% of the world's surface yet hold nearly 30% of the soil carbon, twice as much as in the world's forests. Peatlands are important for catching and storing water, and so reduce both flooding and droughts. Despite their importance, peatlands around the world are rapidly disappearing, but they can be restored over time.

FOR PEAT'S SAKE

Q QUAKERS

"George Fox, one of the founders of the Religious Society of Friends (or Quakers), urged Quakers in 1656 to:

"Be patterns, be examples in all countries, places, islands, nations, wherever you come, that your carriage and life may preach among all sorts of people, and to them; then you will come to walk cheerfully over the world, answering that of God in every one."

Just having hope is too abstract as we face potential catastrophe. Instead, we must act to realise the world we hope for. There's nothing more joyful than living in this way, especially in community."

Every religion has its own approach to answering the challenge of the climate emergency. In 2012, Quakers from around the world pledged, in Kenya, to become "patterns and examples in a 21st century campaign for peace and ecojustice." Quakers have often taken a leadership role in concerns for peace, justice and good stewardship, working with people of all faiths and none.

R RAINFOREST

"Rainforests are an essential part of our global ecosystem. They absorb vast amounts of carbon dioxide from the atmosphere produced all over the world. They are the lungs of the Earth. They also support unknowable millions of species of animals and plants. The rate at which rainforests, especially the Amazon, are being cleared feels utterly incomprehensible. But I know that protecting the rainforest is complicated... There is more immediate income in selling crops, meat and timber. International diplomacy is so vital to saving the rainforest. We need to find ways to value trees in the ground, and to financially support countries with rainforests to let them grow."

In 2021, at COP26, over 100 world leaders signed a pledge to end and reverse deforestation by 2030. The pledge included almost $20bn of public and private funds to support it. As citizens, we need to keep pressure on governments to ensure this pledge is met. We can also avoid companies and products that damage or destroy these wonderful forests.

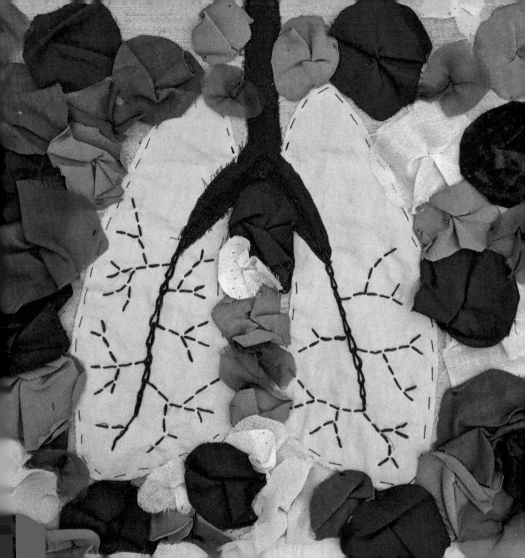

S SYSTEM CHANGE

"Our entire planet is threatened by collapse. These are hard words for me to swallow. My love for this planet and its creatures is infinite. However, the resources we take from it are not. Despite my efforts to limit what I use, I'm aware that huge and brave system change is required... I ask those in power to tell the truth, act now, and let us decide together about our future."

Many aspects of our way of life are contributing to catastrophic environmental damage, and disorder. Some changes have begun, such as investing in renewable energy and developing more sustainable policies, but many vested interests resist such changes, so they are not happening fast or far enough to prevent runaway climate disaster.

Urgent action is needed to tackle this climate emergency. Some people are drawn to carry out non-violent protests to help raise the profile of these issues. Even though they can be disruptive and costly for those involved, activists believe that inaction or superficial changes are much more dangerous for everyone.

SYSTEM CHANGE VIA

NON VIOLENT DIRECT ACTION

T TREES

"Trees are good because they're fun to climb and they give us oxygen and provide homes for birds and lots of creatures. We need to look after them so they can look after us."

Trees are essential parts of many ecosystems around the world. They interact with other species, through exchanges of nutrients and in many other ways. Trees absorb carbon dioxide and sequester carbon through their deep roots. However, trees and forests take time to grow so it's important to care for them and not to cut them down in haste. Mature trees and interconnected areas of wildlife habitats need to be protected so that biodiversity can thrive. Unfortunately climate change is contributing to the spread of many diseases affecting trees. Replacing wild forests with monoculture cash crops (such as palm oil, eucalyptus or cocoa plantations) can be counter-productive, creating new risks of disease or species extinction.

"The best time to plant a tree is 20 years ago. The second best time is now."

—Chinese proverb

U USE YOUR VOTE

"We must use every peaceful means to try to mitigate climate breakdown. Some of the changes we need to make are personal, but governments at all levels need to change too. Everyone who has a vote needs to use it, and we should hold politicians accountable for how their policies and actions affect the whole Earth. We must let them know that we care for the planet and will vote for sustainability and climate justice."

The United Nations' *Peoples' Climate Vote*, published in 2021 found that in 50 countries (covering half the world's population), more than half the population supported conservation, renewable energy, climate-friendly agriculture, and green investments. Public desire for ambitious climate policy isn't always echoed by government actions, but in a democracy, where governments are accountable to their people, we can change this. We can prioritise ecology and environmental justice in political debates and in decisions about who we vote for. We can ask our representatives to speak on our behalf.

BALLOT PAPER

Mark **X** in one box only

OLI DOLLARS
Mining and Extraction Group

MOTHER EARTH
Climate Justice Community Party

MARK E. TING
Greenwash Party

M.E. FIRST
Cronyism Party

OLE HAT
20th Century Hardliners

PENNY PLASTIC
Throwaway Coalition

USE YOUR VOTE!

V VIOLENCE

"Eliminating war is essential to securing the environment. Emissions produced by the military are hard to quantify, but global military emissions are estimated to be of the order of 6%, more than civil aviation. And this doesn't include emissions from war's indirect effects."

Climate change increases the risks of violent conflict. Droughts, or the unsustainable use of water (for example through dam building or diversion of rivers) leads to water shortages downstream and more frequent crop failures, famines, disease and mass movements of people. In turn, these changes can lead to violent conflict and abuses of vulnerable people who can no longer sustain their families.

We need to find better ways to settle our differences, including fairer ways to address migration and access the Earth's resources, prioritising life, equity and flourishing over death and destruction. Could the seeds of war and strife be the same as the seeds of climate change? How can we break the vicious circle?

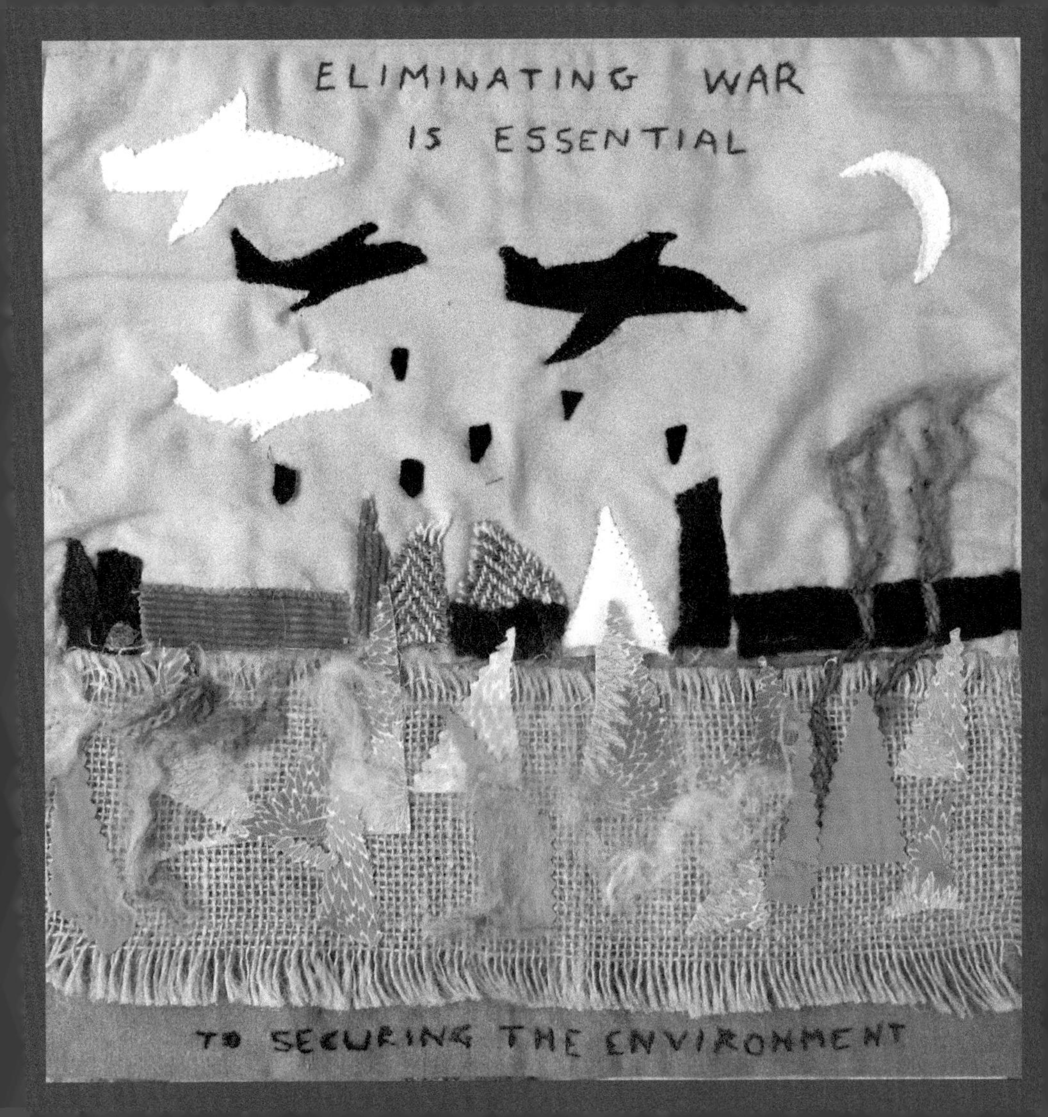
ELIMINATING WAR
IS ESSENTIAL
TO SECURING THE ENVIRONMENT

W WEATHER

"Many people die each year in hurricanes and/or tropical storms, and other animals and plants face deadly conditions during a hurricane. I was recently astonished to discover that one of these devastating storms was named Grace. I wondered what led people to use this unsuitable name! I'm doing what I can to mitigate against climate change, which causes these storms, for future generations' sake."

Our global climate is a complex system; as well as individual extreme weather events, changing weather patterns and rising temperatures are building up to tipping points which will be hard to reverse.

We can feel powerless in the face of these changes, but it is helpful to acknowledge our emotions and to find ways of relating to one another and to the world that are healing and forgiving. The "Work that Reconnects", such as developed by Joanna Macy and Chris Johnstone can help us weather the storms and build resilience for the future.

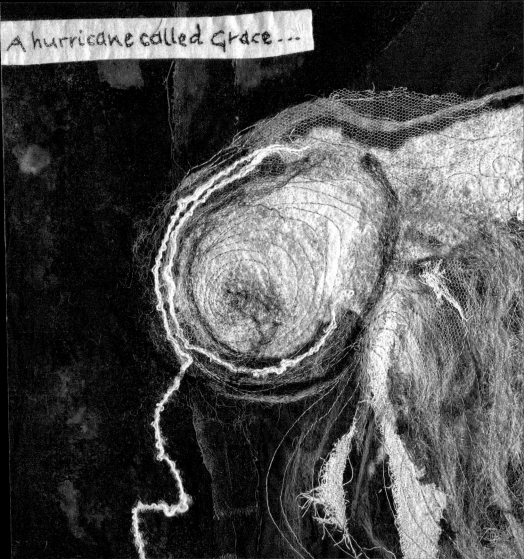

A hurricane called Grace....

X EXTINCTION

"Blessed are the meek for they shall inherit the earth" (Matthew 5:5)

"When I'm honest with myself, my heart is wrung by the thought of the world we're bequeathing to our grandchildren and all the other children in our care. We should be guardians of the earth and future generations; that's part of our day-to-day responsibility. I've decided to ask myself, when I'm contemplating certain expenditures, 'Is this worth contributing to future extinctions, to a less livable world?' I find hope in envisioning our grandchildren as the caretakers we aren't."

Species extinctions occur naturally at a rate of about one to five species lost per year. Currently we're losing species much faster than that, with dozens of species becoming extinct each day on average. That is a monumental loss, to the species, ecosystems, and to future generations. We can engage with legislation to conserve biodiversity, contribute to breeding and seed bank programmes, and purchase sustainable products.

Y YOUTH

"At the start of 2020, the young people in Newcastle Quaker Meeting in England were thinking about climate change and the school strikes. They decided to make fabric panels to celebrate the strikes. Children are worried for their future but don't have much power, except to try to persuade adults to listen to scientists and address the climate emergency urgently. Acting can help to address the climate anxiety that many young people feel acutely. We can all be part of the solution."

"Many say that Sweden is just a small country, and it doesn't matter what we do... but I have learned you are never too small to make a difference. If a few children can get headlines all over the world just by not going to school, then imagine what we could all do together."

—Greta Thunberg.

The power that drives change often comes from surprising places and is cultivated in solidarity with others.

School Strikes
Save our Planet
strike for life
Curtains To Cold! Fight To Prevent Constant
Save our future! You've had your turn. let us have ours
It's OUR FUTURE

Z ZIMBABWE

"Places like Zimbabwe already suffer far more from climate change than my home in Europe does. They are already poor and suffering from droughts, injustice, and famine. We need climate justice, and we need to look after the whole world. That's why I actively support Friends of Hlekweni, which provides education, training, and support for peacebuilding and poverty relief, primarily in southern Matabeleland, Zimbabwe."

Before this century ends, climate change will cause average temperatures to rise by nearly 3°C in Zimbabwe. The country's rainfall, particularly in the south, could decrease by up to 18%, with more severe and frequent droughts, floods, and storms. These changes would have a dramatic impact on any country, but half of Zimbabwe's population already lives below the food poverty line, and over 3 million children there are chronically hungry. Climate change will make relieving poverty much harder. Since our own consumption can drastically worsen others' lives, we have a responsibility to urgently change how we live.

Poverty
Famine
Water
Textiles
Food
Eggs

ZIMBABWE

LOVING EARTH QUESTIONS

These questions are a starting point to help us focus. We can return to them as often as we wish, changing or broadening our focus. We may decide to find out more, and often it is helpful to work with other people.

Think of something you love: a place, a person, a thing:

How will climate change and environmental breakdown affect them? Perhaps it has already?

What actions are needed to reduce the risk of harm?

What will you do to help?

In reflecting on these questions, you may find it helpful to listen to one of the guided meditations on the project's website, at **lovingearth-project.uk**

You are invited to draw, write, or scribble your own responses opposite, or on a larger sheet of paper. If you would like to develop them into a textile panel as part of the project, information about this is also on our website.

WHAT NEXT?

You may want to find out more about some of the issues in this booklet. Searching on the internet can be helpful, especially if you check multiple sources. Some of these are listed on the Loving Earth Project's website.

Intergovernmental Panel on Climate Change (IPCC): This UN body brings together science from across the globe. Specialist reports and summaries can be found at **ipcc.ch**

These have also been summarised by a wide range of other organisations. The Climate Fresk (**climatefresk.org**) offers interactive group exercises to learn about environmental change, based on the science in the IPCC reports.

The UK Government's Climate Change Committee has published several reports advising on the measures that Government should take to meet the UN targets. **theccc.org.uk**

There are many ways to calculate your carbon footprint, to help you work out how you could reduce it. **carbonindependent.org** is a good one.

THE LOVING EARTH PROJECT

The Loving Earth Project was started in 2019 by members of the Quaker Arts Network. Quakerarts.net, an informal group of volunteers set up to encourage use of the arts in Quaker spiritual life and witness. The project has been supported first by other Quaker organisations, then by many other individuals and groups in Britain and beyond. Some of them are listed on the project's website.

Adapting to the Covid-19 pandemic, a number of resources were created for the project's website and many online events have been held. Local events are being organised by a range of groups. Most of the panels were displayed in and around Glasgow in 2021 for the United Nations COP conference, the project was listed among the "best cultural events in Scotland for COP26" (by list.co.uk). The panels are displayed anonymously, and anyone is welcome to join the project, whatever their textile skills or environmental knowledge.

Further exhibitions, other events and publications are being planned during 2022-2023, and all are invited to participate. Our online resources can be adopted for local use; please contact us if you would like advice to organise or publicise an exhibition, host an event, join our mailing list or have other enquiries.

ACKNOWLEDGEMENTS

This booklet was conceived by John Lampen, and edited by members of the Loving Earth Project's Steering Group, and published by the Quaker Arts Network.

Copyright of all images are jointly held by the Loving Earth Project and the panel-maker. We are grateful for financial support from the Westhill Endowment, the Southall Trust, The Edith M Ellis Trust, as well as the Quaker Arts Network and a number of Quaker Meetings and individuals.

lovingearth-project.uk

lovingearthproject@gmail.com

LovingEarthProject

@lovingearthpro1

 Edith M Ellis Trust